DATE DUE   4/17

MAY 3 0 2018			
			PRINTED IN U.S.A.

First Drawings
People

BIG BUDDY
FIRST DRAWINGS
BOOKS

Big Buddy Books
An Imprint of Abdo Publishing
abdopublishing.com

By Katie Lajiness

abdopublishing.com

Published by Abdo Publishing, a division of ABDO, PO Box 398166, Minneapolis, Minnesota 55439.
Copyright © 2017 by Abdo Consulting Group, Inc. International copyrights reserved in all countries. No part
of this book may be reproduced in any form without written permission from the publisher. Big Buddy Books™
is a trademark and logo of Abdo Publishing.

Printed in the United States of America, North Mankato, Minnesota.
092016
012017

THIS BOOK CONTAINS
RECYCLED MATERIALS

Illustrations: Michael Jacobsen/Spectrum Studio
Interior Photos: Deposit Photos

Coordinating Series Editor: Tamara L. Britton
Graphic Design: Taylor Higgins, Maria Hosley

Publisher's Cataloging-in-Publication Data

Names: Lajiness, Katie, author.
Title: People / by Katie Lajiness.
Description: Minneapolis, MN : Abdo Publishing, 2017. | Series: First drawings |
    Includes index.
Identifiers: LCCN 2016945192 | ISBN 9781680785241 (lib. bdg.) |
    ISBN 9781680798845 (ebook)
Subjects: LCSH: Human figure in art--Juvenile literature. | Drawing--Technique--
    Juvenile literature.
Classification: DDC 743.4--dc23
LC record available at http://lccn.loc.gov/2016945192

Table of Contents

Getting Started

Today, you're going to draw people. Not sure you know how to draw? People are easy to **sketch** if you break them down into circles, ovals, rectangles, squares, and triangles.

To begin, you'll need paper, a sharpened pencil, a big eraser, and a flat surface. Draw each shape lightly. When these **guidelines** are light, it is easy to erase and try again.

BASIC SHAPES Circle Oval Rectangle Square Triangle

Baby

Boy

Woman

Man

Grandma

5

Adding Color

Once you learn to draw an object, you may want to add color. Let's learn how to mix colors and add shading.

Shading

MARKERS
Use similar colors to create shading.

PENCILS AND CRAYONS
Use less pressure for lighter shades and more pressure for darker shades.

PAINTS
Add white to lighten and black or blue to darken shades.

There are three primary colors. They are red, yellow, and blue. These colors cannot be made by mixing other colors. However, you can make many colors by mixing primary colors together.

Color mixing

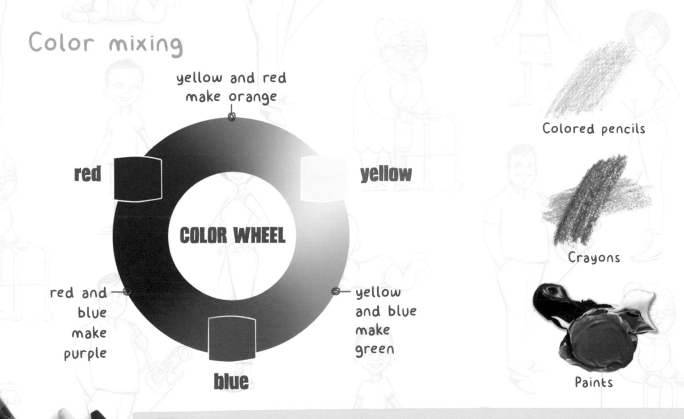

yellow and red make orange

red

yellow

COLOR WHEEL

red and blue make purple

yellow and blue make green

blue

Colored pencils

Crayons

Paints

Tip Create **contrast** by using colors from opposite ends of the color wheel.

Baby

Let's learn to draw a baby!

STEP 1

Draw basic circle and oval **guidelines** for the head, neck, body, arms, legs, and feet.

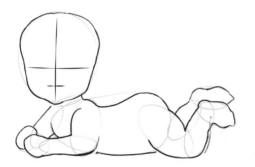

Erase guidelines once you have the parts drawn.

Erase guidelines once you have the parts drawn.

Erase guidelines once you have the parts drawn.

STEP 2

Connect the shapes to form the baby's **outline. Sketch guidelines** across the face.

STEP 3

Fill in eyebrows, eyes, nose, mouth, ears, and hair.

STEP 4

Add the baby's fingers and clothes.

STEP 5

Create **texture** and shape by adding shading.

STEP 6

It's time for some color! You can add your own color and shading to personalize your drawing.

Boy

Let's learn to draw a boy!

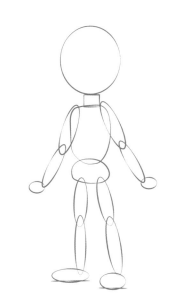

Draw basic circle, square, and oval **guidelines**. These are for the head, neck, body, arms, hands, legs, and feet.

Erase guidelines once you have the parts drawn.

Erase guidelines once you have the parts drawn.

STEP 2

Connect the shapes to form the boy's **outline**. Add his clothes and shoes. **Sketch guidelines** across his face. Draw in his ears.

STEP 3

Add a hairline, eyebrows, eyes, a nose, and a smiling mouth.

STEP 4

Add **details** to the boy's facial features, clothes, and shoes.

STEP 5

Create **texture** and shape by adding shading.

It's time for some color! You can add your own color and shading to personalize your drawing.

YOU DID IT!

Well done! You drew a boy.

Woman

Let's learn to draw a woman!

STEP **1**

Draw basic circle and oval **guidelines** for the head, neck, body, arms, legs, and feet.

Erase guidelines once you have the parts drawn.

Connect the shapes to form the woman's **outline**. Add her hair, clothes, hand, and shoes.

Sketch guidelines across her face.

Erase guidelines once you have the parts drawn.

STEP 4

Draw her eyebrows, eyes, nose, and mouth. Now add **details** to her hands and clothing.

STEP 5

Create **texture** and shape by adding shading.

YOU DID IT!

Congratulations!
You drew a woman.

STEP 6

It's time for some color! You can add your own color and shading to personalize your drawing.

19

Man

Let's learn to draw a man!

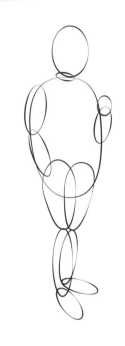

Draw basic oval **guidelines** for the head, neck, body, arms, legs, and feet.

Erase guidelines once you have the parts drawn.

STEP 2

Connect the shapes to form the man's **outline**. Add his hair, ears, and clothes.

STEP 3

Draw **guidelines** for his face.

Erase guidelines once you have the parts drawn.

STEP 4

Draw in his eyebrows, eyes, nose, and mouth. Add the golf bag with a strap.

STEP 5

Create **texture** and shape by adding **details** and shading.

It's time for some color! You can add your own color and shading to personalize your drawing.

YOU DID IT!

Yippee! You drew a man.

Grandma

Let's learn to draw a grandma!

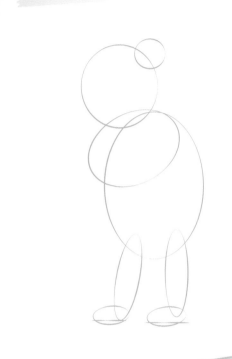

Draw basic circle and oval **guidelines** for the head, body, legs, and feet.

Erase guidelines once you have the parts drawn.

Connect the shapes to form the grandma's **outline**. Add her clothes and hair.

Sketch oval, rectangle, and circle **guidelines** for her arms, hands, and walker.

Erase guidelines once you have the parts drawn.

Connect the shapes to form the arms, hands, and walker **outline**.

Sketch in thumbs and fingers. Draw **guidelines** across the face.

Erase guidelines once you have the parts drawn.

STEP 6

Give her eyebrows, eyes, nose, and mouth. Add a pair of glasses.

STEP 7

Finish any last **details** on her hair and face.

STEP 8

Add **details** to her clothes, shoes, and walker.

STEP 9

Create **texture** and **depth** by adding shading.

Tools There are many tools you can use to add color such as crayons, colored pencils, paints, or markers.

It's time for some color!
You can add your own
color and shading
to personalize your
drawing.

YOU DID IT!

Yay! You drew
a grandma.

To build your drawing skills, practice finding basic shapes in everyday objects. Finding basic shapes can help you draw almost anything. Use what you've learned to draw other people. The more you draw, the better you will be!

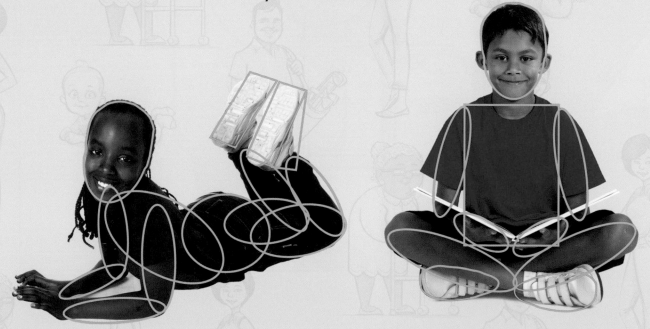

Glossary

contrast the amount of difference in color or brightness.

depth measurement from top to bottom or from front to back.

detail a minor decoration, such as a cat's whiskers.

guideline a rule or instruction that shows or tells how something should be done.

outline the outer edges of a shape.

sketch to make a rough drawing.

texture the look or feel of something.

Websites

To learn more about First Drawings, visit **booklinks.abdopublishing.com**. These links are routinely monitored and updated to provide the most current information available.

Index